Text Formatting

EASY WORD ESSENTIALS 2019

BOOK 1

M.L. HUMPHREY

ISBN: 978-1-63744-058-2

SELECT TITLES BY M.L. HUMPHREY

WORD ESSENTIALS 2019

Word 2019 Beginner

Word 2019 Intermediate

EASY WORD ESSENTIALS 2019

Text Formatting

Page Formatting

Lists

Tables

Track Changes

CONTENTS

Introduction

The *Easy Word Essentials 2019* series of books is designed for those users who just want to learn one specific topic rather than have a more general introduction to Microsoft Word 2019, which is provided in *Word 2019 Beginner* and *Word 2019 Intermediate*.

Each book in this series covers one specific topic such as formatting, tables, or track changes.

I'm going to assume in these books that you have a basic understanding of Microsoft Word. However, this book does include an appendix with basic terminology just in case I use a term that isn't familiar to you or that isn't used the way you're used to.

This entire series of books is written for users of Word 2019. If you have a different version of Word then you might want to read the *Easy Word Essentials* series instead which is written as a more general approach to learning Microsoft Word.

For most introductory topics there won't be much of a difference between the two, but just be aware that this particular series does not worry about compatibility with other versions of Word whereas the more general series does.

Also, just a reminder that the content of this book is directly pulled from *Word 2019 Beginner* and/or *Word 2019 Intermediate* so there may be references in the text that indicate that.

Alright. Now that the preliminaries are out of the way, let's dive in with a discussion of text and paragraph formatting in Word, including how to use Styles and the Format Painter.

Text Formatting

Let's start with a discussion of the basics of text formatting, looking at fonts first.

Fonts

Choosing a Font – General Thoughts

Word 2019 uses Calibri font as the default, but there are hundreds of fonts you can choose from and the font you use will govern the general appearance of the text in your document. Here is a sample of a few of those choices written in each font:

Sans-Serif Font Examples:
Calibri
Arial
Gill Sans MT
Serif Font Examples:
Times New Roman
Garamond
Palatino Linotype

The first three samples are sans-serif fonts. (That just means they don't have little feet at the bottom of the letters.) The second three samples are serif fonts. (They do have those little feet at the bottom of each letter.)

All of these fonts are the same size, but you can see that the different fonts have a different appearance and take up different amounts of space on the page. Arial is darker and taller than Calibri, for example.

Many corporations have a standard font they want you to use to be consistent with their brand and places like literary magazines will often specify which font to use for submitting stories. If that doesn't happen I'd suggest using a serifed font like Garamond or Times New Roman for main body text since a serifed font is supposed to be easier to read. Sans-serif fonts are good for headers or titles or for display text.

Also, unless you're working on a creative project, I'd recommend that you don't get too fancy with your fonts. Certain fonts, like Comic Sans, are so well-known for misuse that they are an immediate indicator that someone doesn't know design or isn't "professional."

The six fonts listed above are ones I'd generally consider safe.

Remember, at the end of the day, the goal is to communicate effectively, which means that a font like Algerian as main body text is not a good idea because readers will focus on the font and not the words.

Font Selection

Okay. So how do you change the font used in your document?

There are a few options.

But before we discuss those, let me point out that if you already know you want to use a different font, it's easier to change the font before you start typing. Once you do so, any new text will be in the new font.

Otherwise you'll need to select all of the text you want to change and then choose your font, which can be tricky if you're using different fonts for your headers and main body text

(A situation like that's also a good time to use Styles which is an intermediate-level topic covered in *Word 2019 Intermediate*.)

The first way to change the font is through the Font section of the Home tab. Click on the arrow to the right of the current font and choose a new one from the dropdown menu.

The first section of the dropdown menu lists the fonts for the theme you're using. Usually that'll be the defaults for Word, in this case, Calibri and Calibri Light.

Next you'll see Recently Used Fonts. (Most of the time there will only be one or two fonts there, but I had used a number recently.)

Finally, below those sections will be an alphabetical listing of all available fonts. If you know the font you want, you can start typing in its name rather than scroll through the entire list. Otherwise, use the scroll bar on the right-hand side or the up and down arrows to move through the list.

Each font is written using that font to give you an idea what it will look like. See for example the difference between Algerian and Garamond above.

The next way to change your font is to right-click and choose Font from the dropdown menu. This will bring up the Font dialogue box. In the top left corner you can choose the font you want.

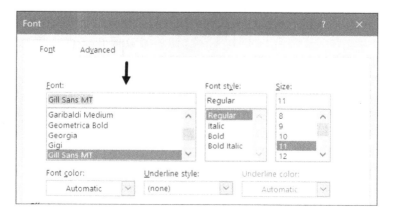

There's a third option for changing the font, something I'm going to call the mini formatting menu. If you highlight your text it will appear on the screen when you let up on the left-click.

It will also appear above or below the dropdown menu if you right-click in your Word document.

As you can see, one of the options that you can change in the mini formatting menu is the font. In the example above, the current font is Arial, but I could click on the arrow on the right-hand side and change that. The dropdown menu looks the exact same as the one from the Font section of the Home tab we saw above.

Regardless of where you choose to change the font, if the font listing is blank that's because you have selected text that contains more than one font.

Font Size

Font size dictates how large the text will be. Here are some examples of different font sizes in Garamond font:

8 point 12 point 16 point

As you can see, the larger the font size, the larger the text for that specific font. Most documents are written in a ten, eleven, or twelve point font size. Often footnotes or endnotes will use eight or nine point size. Chapter headings or title pages will use the larger font sizes.

Whatever font size you do use, try to be consistent between different sections of your document. So all main body text should use just one font size. Same for chapter or section headings.

Changing the font size works much the same way as changing the font. You have the same three options: You can go to the Font section of the Home tab, bring up the mini formatting menu by right-clicking or selecting your text, or bring up the Font dialogue box by right-clicking and choosing Font from the dropdown menu.

If you want to change existing text, you need to select the text first. Otherwise, change the font size before you start typing.

For all three options the current font size is listed to the right of the current font name in the Font section of the Home tab.

If you use the Home tab or the mini formatting menu there is a dropdown list of font sizes to choose from that you can see by clicking on the arrow next to the current font size. In the Font dialogue box that list of choices is already visible in a box under the current value.

If the font size you want isn't one of the choices listed you can type in the value you want instead by clicking into the box that shows the current font size and changing that number to the size you want just like you would with text in the main document.

With the Home tab and the mini formatting menu you can also increase your font size one listed value at a time by using the increase and decrease font options directly to the right of the font size.

These are depicted as the letter A with a small arrow above it that points either upward or downward. The one on the left with the arrow that points upward will increase the font size. The one on the right with the arrow that points downward will decrease the font size.

The values available with that option are the ones in the font size dropdown menu, so you can increase from 14 point to 16 point but not to 15 point using this option.

Font Color

Changing your font color works the same as changing your font or font size. Select the text you want to change and then either go to the Font section of the Home tab, pull up the mini formatting menu, or right-click and choose Font from the dropdown menu to bring up the Font dialogue box.

This time you want to click on the arrow next to the A with the solid colored line under it in the bottom right corner of the Font section:

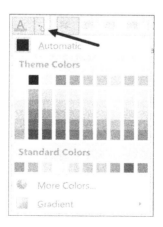

That line is red by default but will change as you use the tool and will stay the mostly recently selected color until you close the document.

Clicking on the dropdown arrow will give you a dropdown menu with seventy different colors to choose from. Simply click on the color you want and it will change your selected text to that color.

If those seventy choices are not enough, you can click on More Colors at the bottom of the dropdown box to bring up the Colors dialogue box where you can choose from even more colors on the Standard tab or specify a color in the Custom tab using RGB or HSL values.

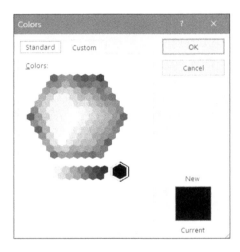

Once you select a font color any new text will be in that color. To go back to the default color choose Automatic from the dropdown menu.

Other Text Formatting

Highlight Text

You can also highlight text much like you might do with a highlighter using the Text Highlighter option which is located to the left of the Font Color option in the Font section of the Home tab or in the mini formatting menu. It has the letters ab and a pen with a colored line underneath.

By default the line is bright yellow but that changes as the tool is used.

To apply highlighting, select the text you want to highlight, and then either click on that option to highlight the text in the currently-displayed color or click on the dropdown arrow and choose from one of the fifteen color choices shown there.

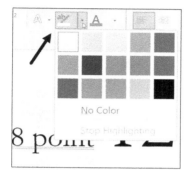

To remove a highlight select the highlighted text, go to the highlight dropdown, and choose the No Color option. Once used, a highlight wil*l not* be applied to new text.

Bold Text

This is one you will probably use often. At least I do. As you can see with the headers in this chapter.

The easiest way to bold text is to use Ctrl + B.

You can use it before you start typing the text you want to bold or on a selection of text that you've chosen.

If you don't want to use the control keys, you can also go to the Font Section of the Home tab and click on the B on the left-hand side.

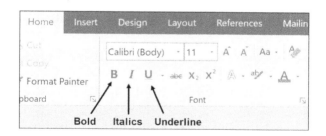

The final option is to select your text, right-click, choose Font from the dropdown menu, and then choose Bold in the Font Style section of the Font dialogue box.

(If you want to both bold and italicize text, you would choose Bold Italic.)

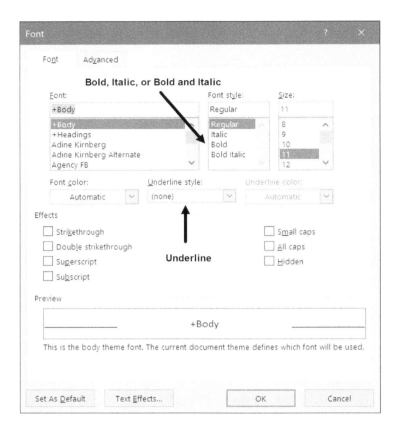

Italicize Text

To place text into italics—that means to have it sloped to the side like the subsection headers in this section for Italicize Text and Underline Text—the easiest way is to use Ctrl + I.

It works the exact same way as bolding text. You can do it before you type the letters or select the text and then use it.

Another option is to click on the slanted capital I in the Font section of the Home tab.

Or if you use the Font dialogue box select Italic under Font Styles. Or Bold Italic to have both italicized and bolded text.

Underline Text

Underlining text works much the same way as bolding or italicizing text.

The simplest way is to use Ctrl + U.

Or in the Font section of the Home tab you can click on the underlined U in the bottom row of the Font section.

There is also an Underline Style dropdown in the Font dialogue box.

Underline is different from italics and bold, however, because there are multiple underline options to choose from.

Using Ctrl + U will provide a single line underline of your text. So will just clicking on the U in the Font section of the Home tab. But if you click on the arrow next to the U in the Font section, you will see seven additional underline options to choose from including dotted and wavy lines.

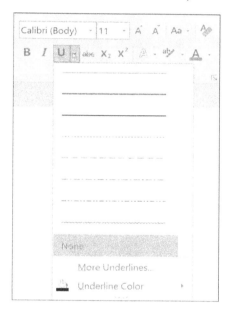

Choosing More Underlines at the bottom of that list of options will open the Font dialogue box where you have a total of sixteen underline styles to choose from.

Remove Bolding, Underlining, or Italics

If you have bolded, underlined, or italicized text and you want to remove that formatting, you can simply select the text and use the command in question to remove that formatting.

So Ctrl + B, I, or U. Or you can click on the letter in the Font section of the Home tab or go to the Font dialogue box and remove the formatting from there.

If you select text that is partially formatted one way and partially formatted another—so say half of it is bolded and half is not—you will need to use the command twice. The first time will apply the formatting to all of the selected text, the second time will remove it from all of the selected text.

Also, with specialty underlining using Ctrl + U will initially revert the type of underlining to the basic single underline. To remove the underline altogether, you'll need to use Ctrl + U a second time.

Copy Formatting

Now for a text formatting trick that has saved me more times than I can count, the Format Painter.

Often in my corporate life I would find myself working on a group document where different sections were formatted differently. Usually it was a subtle difference such as the space between lines in a paragraph. Rather than guess and poke around trying to figure out what was causing the difference, I would use the Format Painter to copy the formatting from a "good" section to the rest of the document.

The Format Painter is located in the Clipboard section of the Home tab.

You can also access it in the mini formatting menu.

What it does is it takes all of the formatting from your selected text and applies it to the text you choose. This means color, font, font size, paragraph spacing, etc. All of it changes.

To use it, select the text with the formatting you want to copy (generally I select a whole paragraph or more), then click on Format Painter, then select the text you want to transfer the formatting to.

You need to use the mouse or trackpad to select the text you want to transfer your formatting to because using the arrow keys or the arrow and shift keys won't work

You'll know that the format painter is ready to transfer the format when you see a little paintbrush next to your cursor as you hover over your document. Format Painter in the Home tab will also be highlighted gray.

To turn it off without using it, use Esc.

If you double-click on the Format Painter it will remain available for use on multiple selections until you hit Esc or start typing in your document or click on it again.

A few more tips:

The format painter can be unreliable if there are different formats in the sample you're taking the formatting from. For example, if part of the text is red and part of the text is bolded and I format sweep from that sample to new text, only the formatting of the first letter in the sample will transfer.

Another issue worth mentioning. Sometimes with paragraph or numbered list formatting, I have to select the paragraph from the bottom instead of from the top in order to get the format painter to carry over the paragraph formatting I want. (This is also why I sometimes select multiple paragraphs.)

It's also possible to sweep formatting that's in one document to another document.

Last but not least, when you copy formatting over, *all* of the formatting in your target text will be removed. This can be an issue if you've used italics or bolding within a paragraph, for example.

That means you may have to go back and put the bold and italic formatting in manually, but sometimes Format Painter is the only way to get paragraphs formatted the same even when they appear to have the exact same settings in place.

Okay, then. On now to a discussion of paragraph formatting.

Paragraph Formatting

What we just discussed was basic text formatting. Now it's time to cover paragraph formatting which includes text alignment, line spacing, the space between paragraphs, indents, etc.

Here we're just going to discuss how to change the formatting of a specific paragraph but once you're comfortable enough in Word, I'd advise that you also learn to use Styles which will let you format one paragraph the way you want it, create a style from that paragraph, and then apply that Style to all other paragraphs that you want to have the same formatting. (It's covered in *Word 2019 Intermediate* or you can learn about it through Word's help function.)

Alright then. Let's talk about how to format a paragraph one element at a time.

Paragraphs

Alignment

There are four choices for paragraph alignment. Left, Center, Right, and Justified. The easiest way to choose your paragraph formatting option is via the Paragraph section of the Home tab. All four options are shown in the bottom row and are formatted to show the alignment they represent.

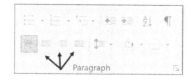

In the image below I've taken the same three-line paragraph and applied each alignment style to it to show the difference between all four using real paragraphs of text:

> This paragraph is **left-aligned**. And now I need to write enough additional text so that you can see what happens when a paragraph falls across multiple lines of text since that can be one of the most significant differences between the choices.
>
> This paragraph is **center-aligned**. And now I need to write enough additional text so that you can see what happens when a paragraph falls across multiple lines of text since that can be one of the most significant differences between the choices.
>
> This paragraph is **right-aligned**. And now I need to write enough additional text so that you can see what happens when a paragraph falls across multiple lines of text since that can be one of the most significant differences between the choices.
>
> This paragraph is **justified**. And now I need to write enough additional text so that you can see what happens when a paragraph falls across multiple lines of text since that can be one of the most significant differences between the choices.

Left-aligned, the first example, is how you'll often see text in documents. The text of each line is lined up along the left-hand side of the page and allowed to end in a jagged line on the right-hand side of the page.

Justified, the last example, is the other common way for text to be presented. Text is still aligned along the left-hand side, but instead of leaving the right-hand side ragged, Word adjusts the spacing between words so that all lines are also aligned along the right-hand side. (That's how the paragraphs in the print version of this book are formatted.)

Centered, the second example, is rarely used for full paragraphs of text like above, but is often used for section headers or titles or quotes. When text is centered the ends of each line are equally distant from the center of the line. You can end up with jagged left and right margins as a result and a final line, like above, may be substantially away from the edges.

Right-aligned, the third example above, is rare for paragraphs, at least in the U.S. and other countries where text goes from left to right. It aligns each line of text along the right-hand side and leaves the left-hand side ragged.

I have seen right-alignment used for text in side margins of non-fiction books and would expect to see it used for languages that read right to left.

So that's the difference between the choices. Like I said, I use Styles or the Home tab to change my paragraph alignment, but there are also control shortcuts that you can use. Ctrl + L will left-align, Ctrl + E will center your text,

Ctrl + R will right-align, and Ctrl + J will justify it. The only one I use enough to have memorized is Ctrl + E.

The third way to change your paragraph alignment is to select your text, right-click, and choose Paragraph from the dropdown menu to bring up the Paragraph dialogue box. The first option within that box is a dropdown where you can choose the alignment type you want. It has the exact same four formatting types that are available in the Home tab.

Spacing of a Single Paragraph

If you've ever attended school in the United States, you've probably been told at some point to submit a five-page paper that's double-spaced with one inch margins. Or if you've ever submitted a short story you were told to use a specific line spacing. In Word this is referred to as Line Spacing. So how do you do it?

As with the other formatting options, you can either do this before you start typing or by selecting the paragraphs you want to change after they've been entered into the document.

Once you're ready, go to the Paragraph section of the Home tab and locate the Line and Paragraph Spacing option. It's to the right of the paragraph alignment options and looks like five lines of text with two big blue up and down arrows on the left-hand side.

Click on the small black arrow to the right of the image to bring up the dropdown menu.

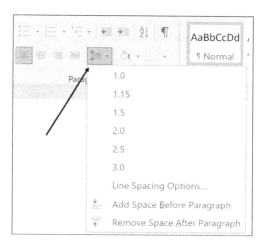

You have a choice of single-spaced (1.0) double-spaced (2.0), or triple-spaced (3.0) as well as 1.15, 1.5, and 2.5 spacing.

Below are examples of single, double, and triple-spaced paragraphs, Note how the amount of space between each row of text increases as you move from single-spaced up to triple-spaced:

> This is a sample paragraph to show you the difference between line spacing. This is a **single-spaced** (1.0) paragraph. I'm going to keep typing so there are three lines of text to help you see the difference.
>
> This is a sample paragraph to show you the difference between line spacing. This
>
> is a **double-spaced** (2.0) paragraph. I'm going to keep typing so there are three
>
> lines of text to help you see the difference.
>
> This is a sample paragraph to show you the difference between line spacing. This
>
> is a **triple-spaced** (1.0) paragraph. I'm going to keep typing so there are three lines
>
> of text to help you see the difference.

If you want a different spacing than one of the dropdown options, then click on Line Spacing Options at the bottom of the list to bring up the Paragraph dialogue box.

You can go straight to the Paragraph dialogue box (shown in the next section) by right-clicking and choosing Paragraph from the dropdown menu. This setting is shown under the heading Line Spacing in the third section of the dialogue box which is labeled Spacing. It is on the right-hand side.

The dropdown menu gives you the choice of Single, 1.5, and Double as well as At Least, Exactly, and Multiple. Multiple lets you enter any value (such as 3 for triple-spacing). At Least and Exactly base the line spacing off of the number of points. So if you have 12 pt text, you can make the line spacing Exactly 12 point as well.

(This is often where I find that in corporate settings someone has tweaked the line spacing on a paragraph so that it doesn't match the rest of the paragraphs in the document. I usually fix it with the Format Painter, but if you don't want to use that, this is another setting to check.)

Okay. On to the spacing between paragraphs.

Spacing Between Paragraphs

There are basically two accepted ways to format paragraphs for most writing. One is what you see in the print version of this book where there are paragraphs without spacing between them but each new paragraph in a section after the first is indented to show that a new paragraph has begun. (Sometimes the first paragraph will also be indented.)

The second option is to start every paragraph on the left-hand side, but to add space between the lines to separate the paragraphs.

By default Word will add spacing between your paragraphs, but you can change the settings so that that does not happen or you can adjust the amount of space that Word adds.

Also, for items like titles or section headers (like you see on this page), it is better to add spacing to separate your text rather than use an extra blank line, because as your document adjusts to new text that extra line here or there can impact the appearance of the document. You may suddenly end up with a blank line on the top of the page that you never wanted there, for example.

And, please, for the love of everything, do not add lines between paragraphs by using enter unless the document is just for you or will only be seen by someone else in a printed format. That's about as bad as using the tab key to indent your paragraphs. (Don't do that either. Use indenting which we'll talk about next.)

Okay, so where do you go to adjust the spacing between your paragraphs? If all you want to do is remove any existing spacing, you can do that in the same dropdown we looked at above. It's the Remove Space After Paragraph option.

If someone has already removed the space after a paragraph and all you want to do is add it back in, you can also use that dropdown and select Add Space After Paragraph. (It's not listed above because there was already a space for the paragraph I was working with, but if your paragraph does not have a space after it, that will be an option you can choose.)

Be careful with the dropdown because it also, as you can see above, can have an Add Space Before Paragraph option. That will put the space above your paragraph as opposed to below it.

For this one, though, I tend to work in the Paragraph dialogue box which you can access by choosing Line Spacing Options in the dropdown or by right-clicking and choosing Paragraph from the dropdown menu in the main workspace:

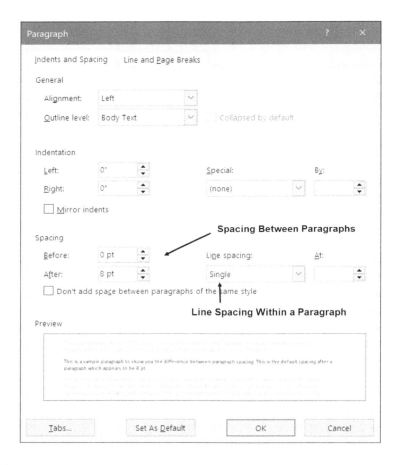

The spacing between paragraphs options are in the third section of the dialogue box, which is labeled Spacing, and on the left-hand side. There is a box for Before and one for After.

If you set your paragraphs to have spacing both before and after, the space between two paragraphs will be the higher of those two values not the combination of them. (So if you say 12 point before and 6 point after, the spacing between them will be 12 point not 18 point.)

If you just wanted spacing at the top of a section of paragraphs or at the bottom of a section of paragraphs but not between them, you can click the box to say don't add spacing to paragraphs of the same style Another option is to just add paragraph spacing to that top-most or bottom-most paragraph (although if you're working with Styles I wouldn't recommend that because you can accidentally override it.)

Below are examples of different paragraph spacing after paragraphs. I have no spacing, the default space that you get from the dropdown which is 8 pt, and 14 pt spacing just to show a visual difference. Because this is a screenshot they may not in fact be 8 and 14 pt spaces, but you can see the relative difference in appearance between each one.

This is a sample paragraph to show you the difference between paragraph spacing. There is **no spacing** after this paragraph.
This is a sample paragraph to show you the difference between paragraph spacing. This is the **default spacing** after a paragraph which appears to be 8 pt.

This is another sample paragraph to show you the difference between paragraph spacing. This time I'm going to put a **14 pt space** after this paragraph.

And this is final paragraph so you can see the spacing above.

Usually if I set a spacing I don't go above the font point size. The above font was 11 point in the document I was using, so in that case my spacing would normally be no more than 11 pt. (If I was writing a large-print document that might not be the case, so know your audience and the standards for that audience.)

Okay. So that was spacing within paragraphs and then spacing between paragraphs. As I mentioned above, if you have no spacing between paragraphs, the standard for indicating a new paragraphs is to add an indent to the first line of each new paragraph. Let's discuss how to do that now.

Indenting

Word provides two indenting options in the Paragraph section of the Home tab, but neither one will not give the first-line indent we need. They move the entire paragraph in or out.

For indenting a single line you need to use the Paragraph dialogue box which can be opened by right-clicking within your document and choosing Paragraph from the dropdown menu.

The second section of the dialogue box is labeled Indentation and covers whole paragraph and single line indents.

The whole paragraph indent options are on the left-hand side. The single-line or hanging indent option (which indents all but the first line of a paragraph) options are on the right-hand side.

Here I have settings for a paragraph with a first line indent:

And here are examples of the various indenting choices:

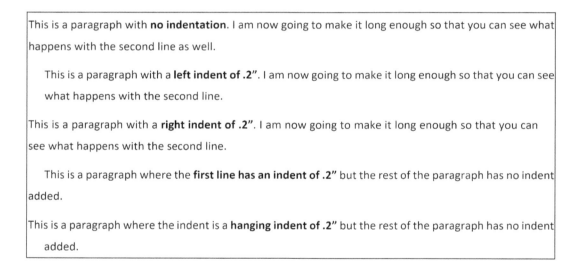

The first example above has no paragraph indent.

The second and third show indents from the left and right-hand sides, respectively. Each is indented by .2" and you can see that on the side where it's indented it either starts or ends earlier than the non-indented paragraph.

(I formatted the paragraphs as Justified so that they'd fit the entire line and make that difference more obvious.)

The fourth example has the first line indented, but the remaining lines would not be. So you can see that "added" on the second line is as far left as the unindented paragraph at the top.

The final example is of a hanging indent where the first line is not indented, but the second and any subsequent lines would be.

To indent an entire paragraph, change the value for Left or Right on the left-hand side of the Indentation section.

To indent just the first line of a paragraph, choose First Line from the dropdown menu under Special on the right-hand side of the Indentation section and then specify by how much in the By box.

To create a hanging indent, choose Hanging from the Special dropdown and then specify the amount in the By box.

Remember to either do this in advance or to select the existing paragraphs you want to change before you start making your changes.

As I mentioned above, there are increase and decrease indent options in the Paragraph section of the Home tab. They're on the top row and show a series of lines with blue arrows pointing either to the left (to decrease an indent) or the right (to increase an indent).

They allow you to increase or decrease the indent for a paragraph or an entire selection of text from the left-hand side.

In my version of Word it indents by .5" the first time, then to a 1" indent the second time, and then to a 1.5" indent the third time.

If there are other indented paragraphs in the document, such as the ones I added before that had a .2" indent, then it will indent to those points as well.

When you decrease the indent it should follow the same stopping points on the way back to zero.

I will often use these quick indent options when dealing with a bulleted or numbered list that I want to visually separate from the main text of my document.

Specialized Text Formatting

I covered basic formatting of text like bold, italics, and underline in *Word 2019 Beginner*, but I didn't cover some of the less common formatting options, so let's do that now.

Strikethrough

If you ever want to keep text but place a line through the middle of it as if someone has come along and stricken it out, you can use strikethrough.

To do so, select the text, go to the Font section of the Home tab, and choose the strikethrough option. It's the one with the letters abc with a line running through them just to the right of the underline option.

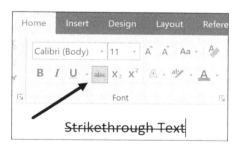

You can also select your text, right-click, choose Font from the dropdown, and then choose Strikethrough from the Effects section of the Font dialogue box. That approach also allows you to choose a double strikethrough option that puts two lines through the text instead of just one.

Subscript Or Superscript

As a refresher, a subscript is when the text is lower than the rest of the text on the line and also generally smaller in appearance. A superscript is when text is higher than the rest of the text on the line and also appears smaller.

The best example of a superscript is the notation for a squared number like we saw above for the equation for the area of a circle which included r^2. Subscripts can come into play when writing chemical compounds like H_2O for water.

If you ever need to do this (for example I have needed superscripts to fix footnotes and endnotes that someone accidentally changed to normal-sized text), select the text you want to format and then go to the Font section of the Home tab.

The two options are located just below where you choose the font size and just to the right of the strikethrough option. They're represented by a small bold x with a 2 in the subscript or superscript position, respectively.

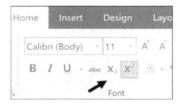

(If you hold your mouse over each one, Word will tell you what they are, what they do, and also what control shortcut to use for them.)

You can also access the subscript or superscript options by selecting your text, right-clicking, and choosing Font from the dropdown menu to bring up the Font dialogue box. The subscript and superscript options are in the Effects section of the Font tab.

Place A Box Around Your Text

This is separate from inserting a table into your document which we'll talk about later. If you just want there to be a box around your text (for a resume, for example), you can click anywhere in the paragraph you want a border around, go to the Paragraph section of the Home tab, click on the Borders dropdown, and choose Outside Borders.

That will place a basic border around your paragraph.

If you select more than one paragraph at once the border will go around all of the paragraphs.

The principles for changing the nature of the box in terms of color and style, etc. are the same here as they are for tables so that's where I'll go into that in more detail.

Place a Border Around Your Page

An extension of placing a border around a paragraph is that you can also place a border around your entire page. Do this by going to the Design tab and clicking on Page Borders to bring up the Borders and Shading dialogue box. For a simple border click on Box on the left-hand side under Setting.

You can play around with the options in that dialogue box to get different page border settings other than the default basic black line.

Place a Colored Background Behind Your Text (Shading)

To add shading behind your text, click on the paragraph or select the text you want shaded, go to the Paragraph section of the Home tab, click on the arrow next to the Shading image (the paint bucket pouring paint in the bottom row on the right side), and choose your color from the dropdown menu.

If you just select part of a word or a single word or part of a line it will look much like the Text Highlight Color option in the Font section.

The difference is in how they handle selecting a whole line or more than one line. Highlight will only highlight where there is text. Shading will color the whole line as you can see in this example.

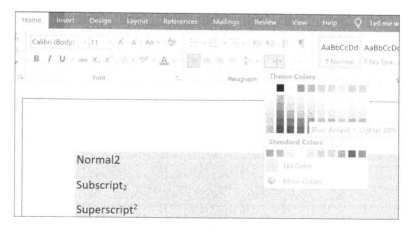

(At the same time, it does not stretch as far as the page border that you can also see as a dotted line in the image above. It limits itself to where text would be.)

Display Text In Multiple Columns

There may be times where you want the text in your document to appear in multiple columns. Think about newspapers, magazines, newsletters, etc. Almost all of those use multiple columns.

To do this you can click anywhere on your text, go to the Page Setup section of the Layout tab, click on the dropdown arrow under Columns, and choose the number of columns you want.

This will apply that number of columns to your entire document. Here I've chosen three columns as an example:

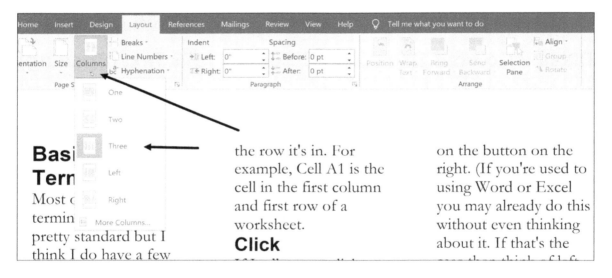

If you only want columns for a subset of your text you can apply them at the paragraph level by selecting just that paragraph or set of paragraphs. This can also be a good time to use Section breaks.

You can see in the screenshot above that your dropdown choices are one, two, or three columns as well as a left column and a right column option. The left and right column options create two columns where either the left or the right column is about half the width of the other column.

If none of those options are what you want, click on More Columns at the bottom of the dropdown menu. This will bring up a Columns dialogue box which allows you to specify the number of columns on the page.

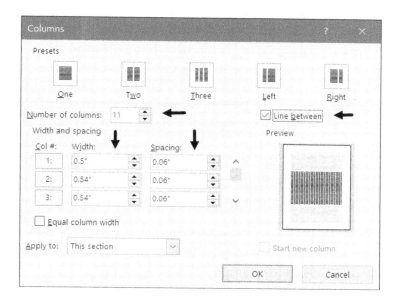

You can also specify the width of each column separately as well as control the amount of space between your columns.

The Line Between option which is located above the preview also allows you to place a physical line between each of the columns.

You can apply the settings to the entire document or just that section.

If you add columns to your document, all of the text will continue down the entire page in the left-most column before moving to the next column on the page and all the way down that column before moving to the next column after that, and so on until all columns have been filled.

As a reminder, if you don't want that—if you want the new column to start with a specific sentence, for example—you can use a column page break to force the text in a column to the next available column.

Add Hyphenation To Your Document

Hyphenation occurs when a word is continued from the current line onto the next line. This is shown by placing a small dash (called a hyphen) at the end of the first part of the word so that the reader knows that the word continues onto the next line.

If you read a lot of books you've probably run across hyphenation and not thought much about it.

It's a good way to have justified text but avoid ugly gaps in a line as Word tries to stretch the text to fit the entire line. This becomes especially important if you like to use big words.

Here's an extreme example of that where I have an incredibly long word. The top example is not using hyphens and you can see that the spacing on that first line is very wide. The second example is using them and you can see how that removes the extra white space between words on that first line because the very lengthy word, supercalifragilisticexpialidocious, is split across lines.

> One of the weirdest words you will ever encounter is supercalifragilisticexpialidocious which I have probably spelled horribly wrong but thankfully spellcheck fixed for me.
>
> One of the weirdest words you will ever encounter is supercalifragilisticexpialidocious which I have probably spelled horribly wrong but thankfully spellcheck fixed for me.

The hyphenation option is located in the Page Setup section of the Layout tab. If you click on Hyphenation you will see a dropdown menu of choices.

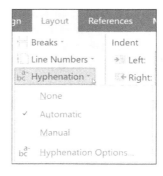

In most instances, the Automatic choice will work just fine. The Manual option allows you to click on a specific word and then choose which syllable to hyphenate that word at. It will apply to every use of that word in your document where hyphenation may be needed,

If you want more control over hyphenation then click on Hyphenation options but the only real choices you have there are whether or not to hyphenate words with all caps and how many consecutive hyphens to allow. The default is no limit, but most formatting guides recommend no more than three in a row.

If you choose to automatically hyphenate, it will hyphenate all of your document. You can exempt a paragraph from hyphenation by right-clicking on the paragraph, choosing Paragraph from the dropdown menu, going to the Line and Page Breaks tab, and clicking on the box next to Don't Hyphenate.

Character Spacing

I tend not to use hyphenation. What I do instead is manually adjust any lines that have a little too much white space in them using the character spacing setting in Word.

To do this, select the paragraph you want to adjust (or the words, you don't have to do the whole paragraph but I usually do), right-click and choose Font from the dropdown menu. From there click over to the Advanced tab and go to the Spacing option.

That option is a dropdown menu that allows you to expand or condense the selected text. I choose condense. Be careful that you don't condense your text too far. I usually won't go above .25 but you'll have to judge things visually because if you're using justified paragraphs it isn't a one-for-one adjustment. You can suddenly have it readjust at .3 or something like that and look better than it did at .1. So you just have to experiment a bit to see what you can do with a particular line.

(Or use hyphenation or a jagged right margin to avoid the issue in the first place.)

Widow/Orphan Control

Another setting you may find yourself wanting to adjust is the widow and orphan control setting. By default Word will have widow and orphan control turned on for your paragraphs.

What this means is that no single line of a paragraph will be left alone either at the bottom of a page or the top of a page. But that can mean that you have two facing pages that don't end at the same point since Word will move that orphaned line to the next page or find a way to keep that widowed line from being alone.

To turn off widow and orphan control, select your text (remember styles, this is probably best done as part of a style), right-click and choose Paragraph from the dropdown menu. This will bring up the Paragraph dialogue box. Go to the Line and Page Breaks tab and uncheck Widow/Orphan control.

(Or if it was turned off and you want it back on, check the box.)

Keep Lines Together

In that same Paragraph dialogue box, you can also manually control a set of lines using the Keep With Next or Keep Lines Together options. This can come in handy at times.

For example, with section headers, I don't want a section header that sits at the bottom of a page by itself without at least one line of the body text to go with it. So part of my style for section headers involves clicking on the Keep With Next option. That ensures that with no effort on my part I'll never have a section header sitting there all by itself at the bottom of a page.

Include a Page Break in the Style

Another option in that Paragraph dialogue box is the Page Break Before option. You can use this one to format a chapter heading style so that Word automatically puts your chapter heading at the top of the next page. It saves the effort of inserting page breaks at every new chapter or section.

(I'm a little too paranoid to use it myself, but it does exist as an option.)

Styles

Styles are one of the most valuable tools in Word. (Maybe right after the Format Painter that was discussed in *Word 2019 Beginner.*)

Styles let you set the formatting for a paragraph once and then apply that formatting to other paragraphs with a simple click. I wrote and formatted *Intermediate Word*, the precursor to this book, in Word and I was able to format the entire book using three styles, one for the chapter headings, one for the first paragraph of a section or chapter, and one for every other paragraph.

Rather than having to remember that I'd indented the paragraph by X amount and had Y line spacing and that it was justified and what the font and font size were, I could just establish that "first paragraph" or "body text" style and then forget about all those settings for the rest of the document.

(For the curious I'm formatting this particular book using a product called Affinity Publisher which also uses styles, but is not Word.)

Okay, so how do you work with styles?

Word by default uses a style called Normal. In my version of Word 2019 that style uses the Calibri font in an 11 point size with left-aligned paragraphs, a line spacing of 1.08, and a space of 8 points after each paragraph. It also includes widow and orphan control meaning that there will not be a single line left alone at the top or bottom of a page if that line is part of a paragraph.

You can see this by looking at the Styles section of the Home tab where the Normal style has a box around it to show that's the current style in use.

To see the current settings for a style, you can right-click and choose Modify from the dropdown menu.

Here you can see that the Normal style is selected and the Modify option is the second in the dropdown menu.

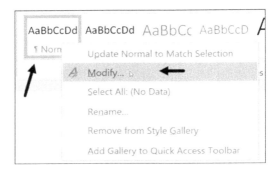

Clicking on Modify will bring up the Modify Style dialogue box which has all of the current settings for that style. We'll look at one of those in a moment.

In the meantime, this is what the Normal style looks like in a document:

> This is a test paragraph so we can see what the Normal paragraph style looks like and how it works when there is more than one line of text. As you can see it left-justifies the text, there is no indent and there is a decent amount of space between lines.
>
> When you start a new paragraph there is a space between the two paragraphs. All of this is part of the Normal style.

I often will write a document using the default style, but I almost never want that style in my final version. (For most non-fiction and fiction the preferred format is to have the paragraphs touching one another and to signal the beginning of a new paragraph by using an indent.)

In addition to the Normal style, Word also provides a number of other pre-formatted styles such as headings, title format, subtitle, emphasis, etc. Each one is formatted in the style section like it will be in the document.

My list of styles displays on two rows. Here is the first row of choices I see with Normal having a gray box that indicates it's the current style in use.

(The number of visible styles may differ for you depending on the zoom level of your screen.)

To see all of the available styles, use the arrows on the right-hand side to move up or down one row of choices at a time.

You can see what each one will look like in your document by holding your mouse over it. When you do that, the paragraph you're currently clicked into will briefly change to show the style.

An obvious example to try this with is the Intense Quote option which colors the text blue, centers it, and puts lines above and below the paragraph.

Here I've gone ahead and applied that style to a paragraph:

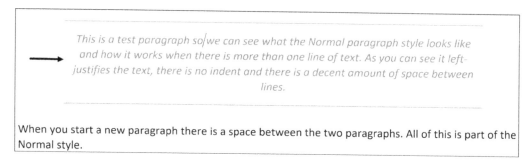

To apply a style, click somewhere on the paragraph you want to format (you don't even have to highlight the whole thing if it's just one paragraph), and then click on the style you want to use.

It's as easy as that.

If you want to see all styles at once, clicking on the down-pointing arrow with a line above it on the right-hand side of the visible styles. That will also give you the Create a Style, Clear Formatting, and Apply Styles choices.

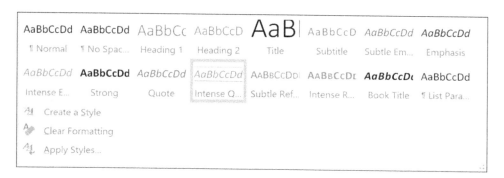

Another point to make about the pre-formatted styles is that using the heading styles (Heading 1, Heading 2, etc.) will also create navigation options that you can use to move throughout your document as well as rearrange your document.

If you have the Navigation pane open (which you can do using Ctrl + F for Find if it isn't already open), click on Headings and you'll see a listing of every text entry that is formatted with one of the heading styles. For example, here I've formatted Introduction and Basic Terminology with the Heading 1 style:

You can click on any of the entries in the Headings section to be taken to that point in the document. You can also click and drag a heading name in that section to a new position in the list and Word will move all of the text for that section to that new location in the document.

(Although be careful with that click and drag option if you're working in a heavily-formatted document. I just did that with the above two sections, clicking and dragging Introduction to after Basic Terminology. Because the document was a hundred-plus pages long and the other chapters weren't formatted using Heading 1, it put the Introduction chapter starting on the same page as the last chapter and with page numbering of 1, 2, 3 even though it was immediately after page 245. Also, because the Basic Terminology chapter was set to continue page numbering, even though it was now the first chapter it was numbered starting at page 11 because of the front matter in the document.)

Okay, so that's how the default styles work. To apply one, highlight the text or click on the paragraph you want to format, go to the Styles section of the Home tab, and click on the style you want.

But the real power comes from creating your own styles.

It only takes setting a style up once and then you can apply that style in all of your documents going forward to create a consistent appearance both within the document in question and across all of your documents.

The easiest way to do this is if there's a style you already like in another document you can use the Format Painter to copy it to a new document. Just highlight a paragraph with the style you want in the first document, click on Format Painter, and then click on a paragraph in the second document to apply the style.

Not only will that paragraph change to that style, but the style will also be added to your list of available styles in the Styles section of the Home tab, which means you can easily apply that style to the rest of the document.

Let's walk through an example of how to apply that style to the rest of the document. Say half of the paragraphs in your existing document are formatted in Awesome Style and you've brought in Even Better Style and applied it to a single paragraph, and now you want to apply it to all of the other paragraphs with Awesome Style.

You do not have to do this individually. You can select all of the paragraphs that are in Awesome Style by right-clicking on Awesome Style from the Home tab and choosing Select All X Instances from the dropdown menu where X is the number of paragraphs in that style in the document. Like here where I have 957 paragraphs in Awesome Style:

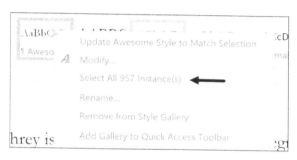

Once you've done that and all paragraphs in that style have been selected, you can simply click on the style you want to apply (Even Better Style in this case) and Word will apply that style to all of those paragraphs.

It takes less than a minute. Although with a big document like I was using here, give it just a few seconds to select all of the paragraphs and then a few more to apply the new style.

(And, no, I don't normally name my styles things like Awesome Style. I just did it for this example using the Rename option you see there in the dropdown.)

So that's one way to apply a new format in your document. Copy it from elsewhere.

But what if you don't have a style to copy? The easiest way to create a custom style is to take one paragraph and format it exactly how you want it. Choose your paragraph spacing, text alignment, font, font size, etc.

Once that's ready, go to the Styles section of the Home tab and at the end of the box that shows the available styles, click on that arrow with a line above it that we talked about earlier to expand the section until you can see the Create a Style option. Click on that and give your style a name.

If you need to make further modifications to the formatting of your new style, right-click on the style name, choose Modify to bring up the Modify Style dialogue box.

Another option for creating a new style is to click on the expansion arrow for the Styles section. This will bring up the Styles dialogue box. The bottom left image in that dialogue box is for New Style.

Clicking on that image will then bring up the Create New Style from Formatting dialogue box.

Basic formatting choices are available on that main screen, but you can also use the Format dropdown list in the bottom left corner to access more dialogue boxes with additional options for Font, Paragraph, Tabs, Border, Language, Frame, and Numbering options as well as a Shortcut Key dialogue box.

The Shortcut key option lets you assign a key sequence to use in your document to apply a format to your paragraph without having to click into the Styles section of the Home tab.

I've found that this can be a significant time saver if I am typing a document with alternating styles, such as this one. Not having to move from the keyboard to my mouse or trackpad saves considerable time.

Just give some thought to your shortcut combo so that it's easy to type. Also, when you add your shortcut Word will tell you if that's already in use or not. Like here where I tried to use Ctrl + Q and it was already listed as in use for some other purpose.

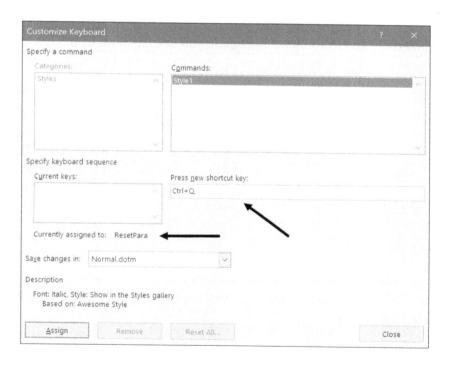

What about an existing style? What if it's close, but not quite where you want it? You can take one instance of that style in your document, format it exactly how you want it, and then go to that style in the Styles section of the Home tab, right-click and choose Update Style to Match Selection from the dropdown.

This will change all instances of that style in your document to the formatting you just used on that one paragraph.

A few more thoughts.

I never edit the Normal style. I don't think it's a good practice to do so, especially since by default your new styles will link to it and so any edit you make to that style will edit any linked styles.

Also, in the new style checkbox you can choose to either have the style you've created available in only that document or to make it available in all other Word documents. (I'm weird so I limit a style to the current document and then use Format Painter to transfer the style to a new document when it's needed. That let's me make sure I'm not having any unintended consequences like updating a style that another style relies upon and messing up some other document accidentally.)

The Manage Styles option, which is the third option in the Styles dialogue box, brings up a Manage Styles dialogue box. In the Set Defaults tab in that dialogue box you can change the default font and font size for Word.

In the Edit tab in that dialogue box you can see all styles that are available for use in Word, including many that do not appear in the Styles section of the Home tab. For example, the Footnote Text style does not appear in the Styles section of the Home tab but can be located and modified this way.

When creating a new style you do also have the option of basing it on an existing style. I've done this, for example, with a document where I have two paragraph styles that are identical except for one attribute, such as paragraph indent. That way when I update one of the styles the other one updates as well.

This can save a lot of time if you're changing the font or font size in a document, for example, and want to easily be able to do so across a number of related styles.

* * *

Alright, then. That's Styles. Incredibly useful once you master them, especially if you create custom styles.

Conclusion

Alright, so that was the basics of text and paragraph formatting in Word 2019. If you get stuck, reach out and I'm happy to help if I can. I don't check email every day, but I do check it regularly.

Good luck with it.

And if you decide that you want to learn more about Microsoft Word or Word 2019, feel free to check out my other books.

Appendix A: Basic Terminology

Below are some basic terms that I use throughout this guide.

Tab

I refer to the menu choices at the top of the screen (File, Home, Insert, Design, Layout, References, Mailings, Review, View, and Help) as tabs.

Click

If I tell you to click on something, that means to use your mouse (or trackpad) to move the arrow on the screen over to a specific location and left-click or right-click on the option. If I don't specify which to use, left-click.

Select or Highlight

If I tell you to select text, that means to highlight that text either by using your mouse or the arrow and shift keys. Selected text is highlighted in gray.

Dropdown Menu

A dropdown menu provides you a list of choices to select from. There are dropdown menus when you right-click in your document workspace as well as for some of the options listed under the tabs at the top of the screen. Each option with a small arrow next to it will have a dropdown menu available.

Expansion Arrows

I refer to the little arrows at the bottom right corner of most of the sections in each tab as expansion arrows. For example, click on the expansion arrow in the Clipboard section of the Home tab and it will open the Clipboard task pane.

Dialogue Box

Dialogue boxes are pop-up boxes that cover specialized settings. They allow the most granular level of control over an option.

Scroll Bar

Scroll bars are on the right-hand side of the workspace and sometimes along the bottom. They allow you to scroll through your document if your text takes up more space than you can see in the workspace.

Arrow

If I ever tell you to arrow to the left or right or up or down, that just means use your arrow keys.

Task Pane

I refer to the panes that sometimes appear to the left, right, and bottom of the main workspace as task panes. By default you should see the Navigation task pane on the left-hand side when you open a new document in Word.

Control Shortcut

I'll occasionally mention control shortcuts that you can use to perform tasks. When I reference them I'll do so by writing it as Ctrl + a capital letter. For example, Save is Ctrl + S.

To use one, hold down the Ctrl key and the letter at the same time.

ABOUT THE AUTHOR

M.L. Humphrey is a former stockbroker with a degree in Economics from Stanford and an MBA from Wharton who has spent close to twenty years as a regulator and consultant in the financial services industry.

You can reach M.L. Humphrey at:

mlhumphreywriter@gmail.com

or at

www.mlhumphrey.com